WORLDLY REVISITED

The Wisdom of Jesus the Son of Sirach

MAX EHRMANN

Edited with a Foreword

by

TIM DALGLEISH

Worldly Wisdom Revisited Foreword by Tim Dalgleish

Copyright © 2018 Tim Dalgleish

All rights reserved. No part of this publication may be reproduced, distributed or transmitted in any form or by any means (including photocopying, recording or other electronic or mechanical methods) without prior written permission of both the copyright owner and publisher, except in the case of brief quotations embodied in critical reviews and certain noncommercial uses permitted by copyright law. For permission requests, contact the author via his website www.lookingfortim.com

All rights reserved

Photo: Izabela Keppler freeimages.com

ISBN: 1987587960
ISBN-13: 978 1987587968

DEDICATION

To my two girls who let me know how it is

CONTENTS

Foreword   3
Tim Dalgleish

Introduction   27
Professor Charles M. Curry

Worldly Wisdom Revisited   31
Max Ehrmann

Appendix: Ecclesiastes   61
Jesus Son of Sirach

About the Editor   87
Tim Dalgleish

ACKNOWLEDGMENTS

Once again DePauw University Archives and its library staff in Greencastle, Indiana, deserve my thanks and appreciation for all their efforts. Wes Wilson, the Coordinator of Archives and Special Collections and his team have endured my requests and questions patiently and always responded swiftly and efficiently. Thanks also are due for permission to publish various materials from the archives including biographical items, letters, items from the press and of course *Worldly Wisdom* itself.

Sarah, my wife, has also been very patient with her impatient husband, and thus improved another of my books with regard to its editorial content. I hope one day to repay her in kind when she publishes her own books.

Foreword

Worldly Wisdom Revisited: The Wisdom of Jesus Son of Sirach was originally called *Worldly Wisdom: Being the Wisdom of Jesus of Sirach* (and in some editions *Faces of Worldly Wisdom*). I have retitled Max Ehrmann's work, in this instance, to draw attention to the fact that this is the first new edition of the work in many years, and also to highlight the fact that this edition is drawn from an original typescript of the work (held by the Depauw University Archives).

Ehrmann's *Wisdom* is itself a *'rendering into verse'*, as he put it on the title page of the typescript, of what is commonly called the book *Ecclesiastes* from the *Bible*. *Ecclesiastes* has been dated as coming from between the 7th and 3rd century BCE. Those who date it from the later 3rd or 4th Century BCE period feel the Hebrew of *Ecclesiastes* is post-biblical, that is after the 6th century BCE, and that hints of Greek peep through. They also perceive the presence of Persian loanwords and some Aramaic. Biblical scholars who are more tempered in their arguments maintain that the distinctive Hebrew of the work is dialectical in nature which circumvents accurate dating.

In the earliest extant Greek manuscripts of *Ecclesiastes*, the book was called *Wisdom of Jesus son of Sirach*. In Vatican manuscripts this became *Wisdom of Sirach* and in the Syriac *Wisdom of Ben Sira*. In the Vulgate (the principle Latin version of the *Bible* prepared by St Jerome in the 4th century CE) the title became *Ecclesiasticus*, then *Ecclesiastes*, and this was adopted for most English versions of the *Bible*.

Other names given to the author and book include Ben Sirach, Shimon ben Yeshua ben Eliezer ben Sira, Jesus Ben Sirach, *Wisdom of Sirach* and the most glorious, *Book of the All-Virtuous Wisdom of Yeshua ben Sira*. In fact, the matter is more complicated still, because the author of *Ecclesiastes* is said to be presenting the *Wisdom of Qoheleth*. Who or what Qoheleth is, is uncertain, it could be a personal name, pseudonym, title or office. In addition to this uncertainty surrounding the etymology of the word itself, the identity of Qoheleth is further cloaked in mystery or distanced by the grammatical 'person' of the text. Qoheleth is initially introduced in the third person, "*'Vanity of vanities'*, saith the Preacher", but even when this changes and the first person is introduced, it is sometimes presented, depending on the translation (it is less true of the *King James Bible* version below), as quoted material. So we have sentences such as, "*'Behold, this have I found'* saith the preacher" which adds to the distancing of the 'voice' communicating the text. There are, in effect, various *personae* within the book.

So in retitling the book, it could be said, I have merely taken up common cause with previous 'editors' and scholars of the text. What's in a name after all? However, the important distinction in this case is that Ehrmann's *Worldly Wisdom* is not simply another translation of *Ecclesiastes* with a new name (but smelling as sweet as all the rest). The truth is it's a new work.

As Charles M. Curry tells us, slightly disingenuously, in his introduction that follows, Ehrmann *'extracted many of the wisdom passages* [from *Ecclesiastes* and]... *In doing this some of the wisdom of Ehrmann has crept into the texture of the poem.'* It might be best then to think of *Worldly Wisdom* as having had a co-authorship or perhaps, as they put it in film credits, one might say, *'Original idea by Jesus Son of Sirach' 'Screenplay by Max Ehrmann'*. The reader can make up their own mind on the issue of authorship, as I have included the *King James Bible* version of *Ecclesiastes* in the appendix, so ancient and modern text can be compared.

I have chosen to include the *King James* version of the poem because I believe, out of the many translations available, this one echoes the style of Ehrmann's verse most closely. Also, it seems likely Ehrmann would have referred to the *King James* translation when composing his own.

Another direct influence on Ehrmann that we can be sure of was a verse translation from Latin of a book called *The Distichs of Cato, A Famous Medieval Textbook*. Sometime after 1922, Ehrmann had been sent a signed copy of this book by its author, Wayland Johnson Chase. Before donating it to Depauw University, Max Ehrmann's wife, Bertha King Ehrmann, wrote on the front page of the book, *'Max studied this for verse forms for* Worldly Wisdom'.

One major similarity between *Ecclesiastes* and *Worldly Wisdom*, is that their authors shared a common unorthodox approach to religious, and specifically Christian, belief. In the case of Jesus Son of Sirach, this is so much so that both the Anglican and Lutheran churches have only a nuanced acceptance of his writings as canonical and Sirach is not part of the Jewish canon at all. An anonymous writer on the *Zondervan Academic Blog*, in October 2017, summed up the situation well:

'The book of Ecclesiastes *has often been avoided by people who feel overwhelmed by the view of life offered in its pages. Like the book of* Job, *it refuses to dodge the hard questions of life and doesn't allow easy solutions. Interpreters of the book struggle with the issues it raises, leading some to question the orthodoxy of the author or whether the book even belongs in the* Old Testament *canon.'*

Max Ehrmann for his part, after a conventional Christian upbringing, gradually lost his faith in Christianity altogether. He maintained, however, a belief in God, '*…whatever you conceive him to be*', as he wrote in *Desiderata* his most famous poem. He believed also in the need for spiritual guidance and wisdom because, as he wrote in his journal,

'To expect God to interfere in one's behalf is to court disappointment - unhappiness. This was Amiel's dilemma [Henri Frédéric Amiel, a Swiss philosopher whom Ehrmann had been reading]. *He believed in God's efficacy; but he could not see any manifestation of God's efficacy because there is not any. Therefore the* Journal Intime *is an endless lamentation so great and so profound that it is almost the complete story of the struggle of the human soul in the meshes of contradictory elements: the hard, indifferent world of the natural order; and a belief in a loving, powerful, fatherly God…*

We must have no malice toward a myth. Nature has one law for all and we can expect nothing of the universe beyond the integrity of nature. Nature may not tell us the whole truth but she represents the conditions of the lease we hold.' (*The Journal of Max Ehrmann*, November 19th 1921)

Wisdom literature for Ehrmann was both a spiritual and *practical* guide to living. One needed counsel on death and the eternal perhaps but equally important was the 'lease' one had on life and the need to live correctly. He passed on such wisdom in his everyday life as much as in his published writing. For instance, in a letter to Henry Boyer Longden, one of his former professors, who was unwell and *'troubled with nerves'*, he wrote:

'Some years ago I made a study of wisdom literature, the result of which was my versification of Jesus Sirach, under the title of Worldly Wisdom, *published in the famous – some think infamous –* Little Blue Book Series. *I noticed in the study of all this wisdom literature the counsel of wine in moderation. I think as one grows older, the wisdom of the ages counsels some liquor.'* (May 19th, 1936, previously unpublished, Depauw University Archives)

Ehrmann's unorthodox book of 'Christian' *Worldly Wisdom* is then a handbook of both spiritual and practical advice. It first appeared, as he notes above, as a *'Little Blue Book'* in 1934. The *Little Blue Books* began appearing from 1919 onwards and lasted until 1978. The series was the work of Emmanuel Haldeman-Julius (1889-1951) and his publishing house, the *Haldeman-Julius Publishing Company*, based in Kansas. These cheap, staple-bound books, were immensely popular in the United States for a time, selling hundreds of millions of copies, appealing as they did to a broad social spectrum of readers. The early names for the series (which were eventually dropped for the less descriptive but more romantic *Little Blue Books* moniker) give some idea of the market Haldeman-Julius was aiming at: the *People's Pocket Series*, the *Appeal Pocket Series* and the *Ten Cent Pocket Series*.

The seed of the idea of publishing with Haldeman-Julius may have been planted in Ehrmann's mind, some years before 1934, by Upton Sinclair. The two writers corresponded briefly, between 1926 and 1931, and Sinclair had ended one of his letters to Ehrmann with, *'It occurs to me to wonder whether you have ever offered any material to Haldeman-Julius.'* The collaboration with Haldeman-Julius certainly gave Ehrmann's long poem a wider audience than he may have gained or expected with another publisher, though this didn't translate into much financial gain on Ehrmann's part. His mixed feelings about this are evident in a report from his local paper, the *Terre Haute Saturday Spectator*, on October 13th 1934, shortly after the book's publication:

'MAX EHRMANN, Terre Haute's internationally known poet, is the author of a new work, Worldly Wisdom, *of which a hundred thousand copies have recently been issued by the* Haldeman-Julius Company, *of Girard, Kan., Publishers of the* Little Blue Books... *The list of authors is extensive, and the series covers ancient and medieval as well as about fifty modern authors. The local poet feels highly-honored to have been included in the series... Some of the newspaper critics think* Worldly Wisdom *a very wise book and believe it is the best thing Mr Ehrmann has done. Mr Ehrmann says the 100,000 edition did not help him much as he was compelled to sell the manuscript outright.'*

Along with his pride at being *'highly-honored'*, one feels a strong sense of chagrin. Clearly there is a realisation that this initial print run is large, and his financial recompense is, relatively speaking, small. However, he would have gained some intellectual solace at how well the book was received by the academic community. Herbert L Creek, Head of the Department of English, at Purdue University, wrote to say he felt,

'... the metrical form which you have chosen seems to be admirably fitted to the substance, and your mastery of it is more than satisfactory.' (October 29th 1934, previously unpublished, Depauw University Archives)

Furthermore, grammaticist Erle Elsworth Clippinger, from the English Department of Ball State Teachers College commented that,

'To catch the spirit and the message of an ancient manuscript of a didactic nature and to make them live in a modern sense is a task for an artist, and it seems to me that you have succeeded admirably.' (October 21st 1934, unpublished, Depauw University Archives).

Part of the reason for this new edition of *Worldly Wisdom* by Max Ehrmann is that certain titles in the *Little Blue Book Series* have now become difficult to get a hold of. This is especially true for non-American readers, who cannot easily come across copies in second-hand bookshops, as they might more readily do in the United States. This is the case even though the first print run was a massive 100,000 copies, which had probably surprised, and then possibly irked him.

Whilst the *Little Blue Books* were very popular during his era with both educated and uneducated readers, the series faced greater competition in America perhaps than say *Penguin Books* in Great Britain. There was certainly a wide range of 'cheap to buy' editions from other publishing houses of the types of books in the series, especially when it came to Classics and practical How-to Manuals. Atypically in this field of publishing however, *Haldeman-Julius* did also venture into more controversial contemporary moral and political issues, such as atheism, homosexuality and contraception. *What Every Girl Should Know* (1922) by Margaret Sanger, on the latter subject, appeared in the *People's Pocket Series*, and would have signalled to Ehrmann that the publisher's outlook was similar to his own, as he himself had written for Sanger's campaigning journal, *The Birth Control Review*, as far back as 1919.

Emanuel Haldeman-Julius, a socialist and political reformer, who wrote half a dozen books, with titles such as *The Militant Agnostic* and *Studies in Rationalism*, was himself a controversial figure. His first by-lined article, *Mark Twain: Radical*, appeared in the *International Socialist Review*, which was published out of Chicago, Illinois (from 1900 to 1918) by Charles H. Kerr & Co. This was at a time when 'Reds' were viewed rather nervously by the American establishment given the Russian revolutions of 1905 and

1917.

Although, by the time *Worldly Wisdom* was published in 1934, Ehrmann could no longer enthusiastically call himself a socialist, he would still have had a residual empathy for some of its tenets. More trivially, it might also have appealed to Ehrmann (who lived in Terre Haute, Indiana, his whole life, and loved his 'neck of the woods'), that Haldeman-Julius had a strong connection with a city only a day's journey from his hometown.

One of the events which had dented Ehrmann's confidence in the socialist cause was undoubtedly his disagreement with Eugene Debs over World War I. Ehrmann would write many articles in support of American involvement in the war, whereas in contrast, Debs had given a speech at a political rally in 1918 denouncing American participation. This had led directly to a ten-year prison sentence for sedition which was later commuted, in 1921, by President Harding.

Debs, who led the way in the formation of the American Railway Union (1893) and the American Socialist Party (1899), had been a friend of Ehrmann for many years before this falling out. In February 1910, as Ray Ginger (one of Debs biographers) tells us, Ehrmann had briefly considered writing a biography of Debs and still, in 1914, one finds Ehrmann being publically quoted as saying:

"Nearly all my life I have lived not far from Mr Debs' home, and for several years I have lived less than two blocks away. Aside from

knowing Mr Debs as a man who has theories about government, I know him as a neighbour. I think he is almost the finest grained man in his private life I have ever known... I should say that this man is loved - here, near his own fire-side, where we know him' (*Eugene Debs: What his neighbours and others say of him*, by James H. Hollingsworth)

Not long after this Ehrmann would see Debs as *'a flaming revolutionist'*, and the more personal element of their friendship was broken. Publically however, and despite their disagreement over the war, there was still much he agreed on politically with Debs, and in *Pearson's Magazine* in May 1918 he wrote:

'He who doubts the sincerity of this man does not know him. He who doubts his power has never heard him... in the homes of hundreds of thousands of workers he is the fearless one, the golden voice, the shepherd of the lowly.'

Though he had preceded this, in the same article, with a rider,

'Like all Idealists, overwhelmed by the barbarities of real life, and carried away by his great loathing of the sham and injustice of it, he sometimes becomes the exaggerator, the misstater, the wrecker, the revolutionist, the false prophet.'

Seven months later, this equivocation over Debs became a confirmed antipathy and an unwillingness to republish an updated version of the article in *The Appleton Cyclopedia of American Biography*. Regarding this change of heart,

Ehrmann wrote to a Mr Leslie at *The Press Association Compilers*, on January 30th 1919:

'I have concluded to withdraw my article on Eugene V. Debs now in your possession. I do this, firstly because in his attitude toward the war he was a help to the enemy. Secondly, because he expressed sympathy and admiration for the I.W.W. [the Industrial Workers of the World, an international labor union, founded in Chicago in 1905], *who[se] platform is violence and revolution. Thirdly, because he has declared himself a revolutionist. And I now believe, had he the power he would endeavour to overthrow the government by force. I fear he has ceased to believe in political democracy. Fourthly, he has declared himself a Bolshevic* [sic], *that is, in favour of industrial control from the bottom up. I believe this kind of socialism impractical and not democratic.'*

On a note attached to this letter, now in the Depauw University Archives, Ehrmann wrote,

'N.B... I did this work gladly [initially] *and without compensation... note how mistaken I was in my explanation in the article regarding his revolutionary tendencies. The last straw to break down my faith utterly was Debs telegram to Clinger etc.'*

In his *Journal*, at the end of the nineteen-thirties, Ehrmann reflected,

'I felt the pain of disillusion when the great-heart Debs, my friend, after preaching love and brotherhood for thirty years, suddenly attempted to provoke a revolution. Revolution! Here in the land of universal suffrage!'

Max Ehrmann unquestioningly loved the country which had seen his family's income grow over a short time, from modest beginnings to ownership of coal mines and then later meat and clothing factories (a small worker's town, Ehrmannville, was even built by them at one point). He'd been employed by his brothers Charles, Albert and Emil, as a credit manager and legal advisor for ten years until he gave it up to write. This Harvard educated ex-lawyer was given a stipend by his siblings to pursue his literary dreams. He always lived modestly in a three-room apartment, and from his thirties on, never struggled to make ends meet in the way Eugene Debs and Theodore Dreiser (another sometime acquaintance of his) or other writers of his generation commonly did.

Consequently, it might be inferred he had a rosier view on life than some of those in his literary, political and social milieu. He certainly became more and more inclined to write on philosophical and spiritual matters rather than political ones as he grew older. Incidentally, Ehrmann was in the habit of sending his work to fellow writers, and there is some evidence he sent a copy of *Worldly Wisdom* to Theodore Dreiser who, like Ehrmann, was born in Terre Haute. Dreiser, famous for introducing a hardnosed naturalism into the American novel, may have appreciated the gift but it's unlikely the quasi-mystical outlook of the book would have appealed to him.

It was not that Ehrmann had no sympathy for someone like Dreiser. Indeed he wrote,

'I often think of Dreiser persisting in an ideal of his art through thirty years of poverty, 'weather-beaten and solitary' *as Mencken described. A flood of gold and the camera came to him at last. Then he did another bold thing: he declared for communism in a country hating it.'* (*The Journal of Max Ehrmann,* May 1ˢᵗ 1932).

The element that was missing in Dreiser's writing was the deep spiritual vein Ehrmann had come to value above all other things. In Ehrmann's eyes, Dreiser's great virtue as a novelist was a determination to dig out and expose the truth in the external facts of his character's lives. Yet for Ehrmann, socialism and the didactic polemic dressed as art, was not enough. When it came to matters of creative endeavour, when it came to *Art*, an injection of the inner spiritual life and a connection to eternal nature was necessary. In one of his poems, he put it this way,

'If you have spoken something beautiful,

Or touched the dead canvas to life…

The God of the universe is your debtor.'

(*If You Have Made Gentler the Churlish World* in *Max Ehrmann's Poems* 1906).

A month after the previous journal entry, he added that in Dreiser's case,

'The facts of the inner life: the whole background of aspirations, exaltations, experience and scholarship unified into a knowing, reposeful personality – to these he is a stranger.' (*The Journal of Max*

Ehrmann, June 6th 1932).

Even though they were born only a year apart, the contrast between the two writers experience of Terre Haute in childhood could not have been starker. Although there were many similarities in their background, the dissimilarities perhaps made all the difference to their future outlook.

John Paul Dreiser, Theodore Dreiser's father, was an unlucky man, whom fate made *'a morose and dour figure, forlorn and despondent'*, as his son later described him (Philip L Gerber, *Theodore Dreiser*, 1964). One instance of the poor luck Dreiser Sr. had, occurred in 1870, a year before Theodore's birth, when *'a trio of misfortunes struck in rapid sequence…'* (Gerber).

The German-born John Dreiser had, twenty-five years after entering the United States, finally worked his way up to running a woollen mill. In 1870 it burned to the ground. In the process of rebuilding the mill, a second accident added to his misfortunes when a beam fell and severely injured him (permanently destroying the hearing in one ear). The final calamity occurred as he lay convalescing. Sarah Dreiser, John's wife, was cheated out of the rest of the family's property by, what John Dreiser would always call, *'Yankee trickery'*.

The consequences of these events on Theodore's early life were dramatic. For many years the Dreisers were constantly on the move and very nearly destitute. More often than not, Sarah would open a cheap boarding house, only to see the venture fail and the family be forced to relocate. As Philip Gerber says, in his book on Dreiser, *'In Terre Haute alone the Dreisers resided in at least five or six houses, each inferior to the one before.'*

The one chink of light in Theodore's early life (and strong impetus to his becoming a novelist) was provided by his older brother Paul. Paul Dresser (he changed his name to make it sound more American) had runaway from home at fifteen to join a traveling minstrel show (*'Hamlin's Wizard Oil'* outfit as Erhmann called it, see below), afterwards becoming highly successful as a vaudevillian and writer of sentimental and comic tunes such as *On the Banks of the Wabash*, *My Gal Sal* and others. Paul returned home after a four-year absence with what Gerber describes as *'the irruptive impact of a* deus ex machina'.

Interestingly, when Ehrmann wrote of Dresser's life (in *Paul Dresser composer of 'On the Banks of the Wabash'* 1924), he romanticized Dresser's story as being one of a 'rags to riches' affair. Rather than mention the rapid rise of industrialisation and prostitution in old Terre Haute, he begins his account by talking of the natural beauty of Terre Haute and its environs, *'Always and everywhere rivers have been a charm and delight'* he intones. Ehrmann enlisted Theodore's aid when writing the piece, and in his letters to Theodore, seemed very interested in the house the family grew up in. To name only one address in this context is in itself, as we've seen, a bit of a fiction. Nonetheless, Ehrmann continued eulogistically (one might say euphemistically) with regard to the Dreiser's home,

'He was born April 23, 1857, on Walnut Street, Terre Haute, Indiana. The house still stands. It is a block and a half from the Wabash River, which was among the first things that his boyish eyes looked upon. His first little journeys in the world were down to the river to see the boats load and unload. That was in the days of the Civil War. He saw the soldiers come and go. The Wabash was to him the world.'

It all sounds like an almost antebellum idyll. It certainly doesn't have the postbellum chill that Theodore himself evoked when he said that thinking of his childhood days always made him shudder with *'an indefinable and highly oppressive dread.'* As Gerber says, *'To be destitute* [as the Dreisers were] *in winter was a threat to survival itself. Food, shelter, heat, heavy clothing to cope with biting Midwestern cold: these were the needs.'* Ironically, one of those 'needs' was provided to Midwesterners at the time by the Ehrmann Manufacturing Company. Howard Meredith Ehrmann, Max Ehrmann's nephew, recalled in later years that the company made various items of clothing but *'...the one I admired [was] the '1815' ... which was a very heavy, very sturdy blue denim overall with rivets at the corners of all the pockets. [They were] highly reinforced... The brand... was called the 'Never-Wear-Out' brand, and I don't believe '1815' wore out.'* (Interview tape, Jane Hazeldine, Vigo County Library Oral History Program, 1980). The '1815' was just the kind of item, one supposes, that the Dreisers wouldn't have been able to afford.

Unlike Ehrmann, who always looked back fondly on his school days, Theodore Dreiser had a hard time in a series of parochial schools which he was apt to compare to prisons. Of the various pastors he came across in his younger years, the following description of one in particular, represents what he felt about them in general: '[He was] *a low-browed dogmatic little Bavarian, panoplied with the trashy authority of his church.*'

These events and others left Theodore Dreiser with a permanent sense that most lives hang in a fateful balance between triumph and disaster, but also that the established moral codes and society were *'a curse to the individual'*.

In its earliest years, the Ehrmann family had been relatively poor, but they never suffered the severe deprivations the Dreisers had. Max's was a relaxed and loving household, which he always, and frequently, recalled with deep affection. A typical example of this can be seen in his poem, *Thou Mother*:

Thou mother of my childhood's pleasant days,

Still whispering hope and courage through the years,

In stilly cooling eve and daylight's rays,

Art thou naught but a vision bringing cheers?

Or dost thou walk with me along the ways,

And know my inmost joys and my dread fears

That pass when thou art near and far-off seem?

This first appeared in *Max Ehrmann's Poems* published in 1906. He rewrote the poem decades later, and a revised version called *Mother*, was published posthumously in 1948 by his wife, in *The Poems of Max Ehrmann*. The revised version goes thus:

'O mother of my childhood's pleasant days,

Still whispering courage and dispelling fears,

Are you a dream come from my younger years,

And know my triumphs or my inner tears,

That quickly cease when you close by me seem?

Let me sleep on, dear God, if I but dream.'

Clearly he is still haunted, and comforted, by the memory of his mother and his childhood. This again is in naked contrast to Dreiser, who only in his mature years softened towards his father, saying, he was *'... a poor, tottering, broken soul wandering distrait and forlorn amid a storm of difficulties: age, the death of his wife, the flight of his children, doubt as to their salvation, poverty, a declining health.'*

Max's parents were Methodists, who had left Germany (separately) after the 1848 Revolution with little more than dreams of a new life. However, with luck, effort and fortitude, Maximillian Ehrmann, Max's father, had initially on his own, then collectively with the aid of his older boys and daughter Matilda, worked the family up into a position of some wealth and influence in Terre Haute. Whilst Max always made a point of mentioning ordinary working class people in his writing, such as those who might have been employed in his family's businesses, nonetheless, he did not empathise directly or whole heartedly with working-class culture. He always maintained what one might call a paternalist stance towards working people.

Rather like Eugene Debs, who, in his earliest years at least,

'Harkened back to the Terre Haute of his youth… the harmonious relationships… that developed in old Terre Haute… everybody he [Debs] said, could aspire to do something good in their lives whether you be a business owner, whether you're a worker… everybody had the chance… to do something… to improve their lives and that's what he held in most regard in terms of his upbringing.' (Professor Lisa Phillips on the documentary *Eugene Debs – C-SPAN: The Contenders*, 2012)

For Debs, this sentimental attitude toward Terre Haute and his upbringing, changed; for Ehrmann it never did. Even when, in 1913, his brother Emil shot and killed a teamster (who had attacked him during a strike at one of the Ehrmann factories in Terre Haute) Max maintained a sympathetic and benign, if distanced, view of working people.

Again, unlike and in contrast to Dreiser, (who ended his

brief time at Indiana University - between 1889 and 1890 - abruptly, by refusing to go to the end of term's *'silly revelries'* and saying without a backward glance, *'They can all go to hell!'*), Ehrmann had a jolly time at university (Depauw and Harvard) being active in his Fraternity, *Delta Tau Delta*, and editing student magazines.

Max, the youngest in his family, was fortunate enough to be classically educated by some of the greatest philosophers of the era. William James, Josiah Royce and George Santayana were all professors at Harvard during his time there. This left its mark.

Like Josiah Royce, Ehrmann believed we all seek a cause beyond ourselves, that meaning lay beyond the everyday world. Much of Ehrmann's work is suffused with the desire to reach for 'higher things'. Equally, he drew inspiration from the work of William James and his notion of 'pragmatism'. The pragmatist felt that ideas and beliefs were not inherently true but were made true by their practical consequences. If religious or artistic beliefs had efficacy for the holder of those beliefs then even in the modern world of democracy, rationalism and scientific advance, the individual could carve out their own belief system. In 1920, in an essay called *The Malady of Romanticism*, which rails against *'modern fiction… and the moving picture'* Ehrmann writes:

'I am in favor of Democracy in politics. I believe the people have the inalienable right to choose their officers and their government. I believe

in political democracy. I also believe in a kind of industrial democracy. But I cry out with my full strength against democracy in art; against the popular tyranny which says that only that kind of artistic thing shall be created which fits the still benighted citizens of Philistia. I protest with all my voice against the masses choosing my reading matter for me!'

One should be careful not to read this as a 'blanket ban' by Ehrmann on all popular culture. Certainly, he was happy to give praise to popular films if they reached a high enough standard. For instance, in January 1916 he was asked his opinion (by his local paper the *Terre Haute Daily Tribune*) of DW Griffith's film *The Birth of a Nation*. This classic of early cinema has troubled later generations with its depiction of the Ku Klux Klan in ways that hardly occurred to commentators at the time. Ehrmann, like many others at that point in history, fully endorsed the films artistic merits and was quoted by the *Tribune* as saying, *'I am thankful to have lived long enough to have witnessed this marvelous achievement in theatricals. To me* Birth of a Nation *is the supreme wonder of the period.'*

In the previous year he had praised a film which has worn less well, George Kleine's spectacular *The Last Days of Pompeii* (from a novel by Lord Bulwer-Lytton). *'I would enjoy seeing this picture at least twice every year. It is a picture that will never grow old. The superb acting of the blind girl Nydia, the gladiatorial combats, the eruption of Mt. Vesuvius and other spectacular scenes, make it a twentieth-century masterpiece.'* (*Terre Haute Daily Tribune*, October 15th 1915)

Obviously, and perhaps despite his better judgement, he enjoyed the epic grandeur and the dramatic punch cinema could sometimes deliver. Presumably, he felt the uplifting nature of such material, especially if based on classical material of some sort, provided a practical fillip to the soul.

By 1927, when he writes *Lifting the Veil*, an investigation into what lies beyond the material world, his prose is a cross - as George Bicknell called it - between *'the philosophy of Jesus and Nietzsche'*. The citizens of Philistia having been left far behind as possible. Ehrmann wrote, or rather adapted, the verses of Jesus Son of Sirach, in 1933-4, believing a spiritual life was the highest life toward which one could orientate oneself. He did not reject Natural Science, but it was merely an ally in the investigation of spiritual matters. Early in life, he had gently rejected the Christian God of his parents. He enjoyed the wisdom he found in the *Bible*, and many of its adherents, but ultimately he rejected any, and all, churches. Their *'ugly idea of the WHOLE TRUTH, the ONE TRUTH,* [and] *the 'ABSOLUTE TRUTH'* (*Journal*, April 13th 1919) was especially questioned by him in the aftermath of the mass killings of World War I.

In the same *Journal* entry as quoted above, he writes,

'Religion is an absolutistic metaphysics, and explanation of the world by one set of principles. If this set of principles is true, how can there be any truth outside it?... Is it not a more liveable principle that there may be many TRUTHS, all valuable for the purposes of living?'

Note then, that when Professor Charles M. Curry writes in the introduction that follows, '...*some of the wisdom of Ehrmann has crept into* [the texture of] *the poem'*, what he is indicating is this tendency toward what Thomas Paine would have called Deism or we might, in contemporary terms, call a general, pluralistic spirituality. There may even be a hint of pantheism in Ehrmann's lifelong love of nature and the night sky. We can see this 'push' against the religions of the book and a desire to see God in nature in his poem *Revelation*,

'Once I stood in the still night upon the shore of a lake;

and for a long time I watched the lurid west.

I saw God painting upon the sky-curtain of the softening dark.

The moon and her brood of stars wandered through the night.

And I said to myself, "I need no bibles of old revelation;

out of this beauty is my faith born."'

In the end, and despite his source material for *Worldly Wisdom* being from a *'bible of old revelation'*, Max Ehrmann gave credence neither to creed nor the legislation of 'The Word'. His true allegiance was not left-wing politics or social harmony, although he believed in both, but to the spirit of *gnosis* and the broader interpretation of all religious thought. His faith was, as Aldous Huxley and others have called it, a faith in the *'perennial truth'*.

Note: This edition of *Worldly Wisdom* has been produced from the original typescript of the book (see note below) held by the Depauw University Archives rather than from the 1934 *Little Blue Book* edition of the work. Any differences between this and the *Little Blue Book* edition are due to this circumstance. Also, text which appears between square brackets in the following introduction, indicates material that Professor Curry (or Max Ehrmann) originally exorcised. I have chosen to reinstate this, as I thought the deleted text was of interest.

Introduction

'I should like to see a critique of common sense' once said Goethe. Here is one. Wisdom, over two thousand years old, contains the rules of successful practical living as if it had been written today. A modern historian has declared it as *'the sanctification of common sense'*. Who was its author, Jesus, the son of Sirach? No one knows. Whoever he was, he understood how to play the game of life. For two hundred years after the second century, this book was a part of the Christian canon. [The Jews also read it, but they made it no part of their sacred writ, perhaps because of its Greek artistry. It is true also that] Each nation, religion and age interpolated it for its own purposes. This is thought to be especially true of the Greek and Latin manuscripts. So that this apocryphal book, this *Ecclesiastes,* is a compound of some spurious matter and much superb wisdom.

Mr Ehrmann has extracted many of the wisdom passages, which are without doubt the genuine passages of the book, and has turned them into verse. In doing this, some of the wisdom of Ehrmann has crept into [the texture of] the poem. Yet he has remarkably kept faith with the thought and language of the Son of Sirach.

[Has human nature changed in over two thousand years? It seems not. Wisdom might have been written today]. Wisdom deals little with metaphysical problems, such as

Fitzgerald dealt with in Omar, or Burton in *The Kasidah*. It is not at all interested in the philosophical *'whichness of the what'*, of life or the after-life. Here is a world, a fairly acceptable one, and Jesus Son of Sirach tells us how to get the most out of it and his advice is quite different than Omar's. The Son of Sirach did not sit in an ivory tower and copy models of literature. He was on the street and copied life. He evidently lived to a great age and tasted of all the fruits of life. He tells us which are bitter and which are sweet.

I do not know anywhere else where there may be found such worldly wisdom. [He knows nothing and cares nothing about any heaven or hell. His interest is in this world, and to him, this world must justify itself. To be well-bred, well-to-do, healthy, and to live simply and a long time, are his ideals.] He believes in the prudential life. [Life as an art may be considered as a dance, according to Havelock Ellis. But Life is more like science, and deals with careful and industrious walking; and the Son of Sirach would say, *'Watch your step'*.] As was said in the parable of the unjust steward, *'The children of this world are wiser... than the children of the light.'* Jesus, the Son of Sirach, was a child of this world. [So are they of the present generation. But the present generation has not yet found a guiding principle. Everybody is so free that there is no freedom. Satiety seems to be the true success. Therefore] Wisdom is as pat today as it was two thousand years ago.

[Mr Ehrmann's craftsmanship is here at its best for this

book, and Mr Ehrmann has succeeded admirably in imprisoning much of it within these verses.]

Charles M. Curry

Professor of Literature

Indiana State Normal School*

*n.b. former name of Indiana State University, ed.

WORLDLY WISDOM REVISITED

The Wisdom of Jesus the Son of Sirach

I

O hear me, all you great and all you underlings,
My sons and daughters, hear the gifts that wisdom brings!
Long have I lived, experienced much,
And pondered deeply many things.

II

A wise man's knowledge often saves him subtle harm.
He wears his wisdom stately as a golden charm;
And wisdom finally clings to him,
A jewelled bracelet on his arm.

III

Gather instruction from your youth; and on each page
Read well the writ, that you be wise in your old age.
How many laughing lips at dawn
At evening twilight curse and rage!

IV

When men of understanding speak, your tongue you hold;
Bend down your ear, much wisdom will the earth unfold.
Mad men run for this thing, that thing.
Far better wisdom than much gold.

V

For wisdom will receive a man as does a bride;
She give him joy and strengthens him for tasks untried.
From ripened fields she brings him bread,
And cooling drink from mountain side.

VI

Beware of gifts. They blind the eyes and bind the tongue.
What profit is your wisdom in a corner flung?
Let the foolish hide their folly;
But the mouth of wisdom be unstrung.

VII

Much time for study brings out wisdom round and full
What time for learning has the man who shears the wool,
Who plants and reaps and fattens cows,
Whose endless talk is of his bull?

VIII

Shall iron-smiths and carpenters the people rule?
Or potters, gravers, men who work upon a stool?
Where has the toiler learned to guide
The council? Has he been to school?

IX

Each in his craft is skilled and does a useful part;
But woe to the nation tearing learning from its heart,
And crushing learning underneath
The stumbling feet of shop and mart!

X

That soldiers who have fought in battle suffer need,
And learned men be spat upon as if a weed –
These things shall make thee grieve and fear;
These things shall make a nation bleed.

XI

For things beyond your mind and muscle never plot,
Neither curious things unnecessary to your lot.
Now many shout opinions vain,
Professing knowledge they have not!

XII

Strive not with him who is all tongue, or him a liar,
Jest never with a ruffian to rouse his ire.
In heat of summer will a man
Heap wool upon a useless fire?

XIII

Strive not at all in matters that concern you not;
Nor meddle much; enough of problems you have got.
But once engaged, hear all men out;
Decide not while the talk is hot.

XIV

Chide not your father in his age for length of years,
His understanding gone, his eyes oft moist with tears.
Despise him not in your full strength,
Lest one day these be your own fears.

XV

Has fate denied you many children? Do not sigh,
Far better one of sense than fools a thousand high.
Strong men and wise shall cities sire.
The children of the weakling die

XVI

A horse not broken well will soon become high-strung.
A child unchecked restraint unto the winds has flung.
Upon his follies do not wink;
Bow down his neck while he is young.

XVII

Whene'er your elders speak, give an attentive ear.
They learned of their forebears. Thus teach your sons to hear.
Ah, youth is full of golden dreams!
But golden dreams are things to fear.

XVIII

Speak, young man, if there be need; but let your speech be brief.
Where great men are, pose not as equal to the chief;
For favours follow modesty.
In youth proud speaking come to grief.

XIX

O youth, burn not yourself on false ambitions flame!
No treasure compensates the galling sense of shame;
For life is hard with bad repute;
But pleasant with a gracious name.

XX

O youth, the flower of your tender age keep sound.
Beware, sow not your strength upon a stranger's ground;
So may your race be magnified,
A race that has no hidden wound.

XXI

What is more wicked than a covetous man; for such
Puts up his soul for sale, and says, *'How much, how much?'*
His heart is cold like snow on Hermon,
His fingers have an icy touch.

XXII

Be watchful of the rich that evil are. They bend
And smile, and put your heart in hope of some good end.
Beware. Meantime they draw you dry;
Yet cringing ask, *'What wouldst thou, friend?'*

XXIII

A rich man bids you come. Be watchful of his sway,
Lest he be evil. Stand not close nor far away,
Believing little of his talk,
Nor your own secret heart betray.

XXIV

Have lamb and world each other ever understood?
Was ever formed a dog-hyena brotherhood?
The wild ass is the lion's prey,
So are the poor the rich man's food.

XXV

What sticks betwixt two stones as firmly as a pin!
Just so twixt buying and selling sticks much subtle sin.
Whoever has to do with merchants
Surely will be taken in?

XXVI

Whoe'er engages laborers in cunning strife
To swindle them, he cuts them down as with a knife.
Who swindle surely murders them,
For to the needy bread is life.

XXVII

Who greatly loves much gold shall not be justified.
Who seeks much gold by violence shall be denied;
Of violence the horror know.
Ah, many have this folly tried!

XXVIII

The rich man labors hard his money bags to fill.
Ah, but he has of meats and sweets whate'er he will!
Who has no capital labors much;
Night falls and he has nothing still.

XXIX

Defraud no poor man, do not make his portion less;
Add not more trouble to a woman in distress.
Instead of husband to their mother,
Be father to their fatherless.

XXX

A gift is vile, but pleasant words shall make it meet.
Whatever gift you give with pleasant words make sweet.
A truly gracious man gives both,
Just as the dew assuages heat.

XXXI

The rich complains, 'I get no thanks for my good deeds.
E'en he speaks ill of me who at my table feeds.'
How oft shall he be laughed to scorn!
The world not much of praise concedes.

XXXII

Who gathers in much gold his peace of soul will rend;
At every turn a rich man must his wealth defend.
He wearies and he passes out,
And what he had mere strangers spend.

XXXIII

Gaze not upon a maid, to fret yourself and sigh.
Avoid artistic women; many tricks they try.
Unto no wanton give your soul,
To steal your money and to fly.

XXXIV

Look not around about you in the city streets,
Nor solitary places where one pastime meets.
There is the wormy husk of love,
The love that like a fire eats.

XXXV

Look not upon a woman's beauty with desire,
Nor sits at wine and wives of other men admire;
For beauty is a cunning thing,
And drinking kindles like a fire.

XXXVI

Look little on the finery of woman's dress.
Nor sit with them in their resplendent idleness.
They seek to rouse in you desire;
Then pride themselves on your distress.

XXXVII

Now pleasant sin! But flee it as a serpent's face.
It bites as do the lion's teeth. Its firm embrace
Is death. It is a two-edged sword
That slashes down a foolish race.

XXXVIII

Who will not notice little things shall fall by them.
And wine and women fill the clearest head with phlegm;
For morning's pleasure stales by noon;
By evening moths and worms contemn.

XXXIX

If madly you pursue a passion mile on mile,
You flirt with death; and they who watch will only smile.
Who pleasure finds in much 'good cheer'
Has but a very little while.

XL

None knows how oft a father watches in the night,
And trouble o'er his daughter by the candlelight,
In girlhood lest she be defiled,
And lest her marriage be a blight.

XLI

Who sponges off another lives as in the mire.
No self-respecting man will such a life desire.
Begged meat is sweet within the mouth,
But in the belly it is fire.

XLII

Better a poor man's cottage without fear and doubt,
Than miserably from house to house to toss about.
At any hour the host may say,
'Stranger, I want my house, get out!'

XLIII

Bring home not every man you find when it grows dark,
Lest evil ones, thief-like, your every movement mark.
For man has many plots. A heap
Of coals is kindled of a spark.

XLIV

The beauty of a woman and her soothing voice
Are a help and a place of rest to make a man rejoice.
She is a house inside a hedge.
Her husband stays at home of choice.

XLV

But he that has no wife will wander up and down;
For who will trust a thief that skips from town to town,
And who believe a man that sleeps
Wher'er he is when night comes down!

XLVI

As age grows weary climbing up a sandy hill,
So, too, a quiet man whose wife is never still.
Is your wife rich? Then cease to work,
If you would her affection kill.

XLVII

A wife who does not soothe her husband in distress,
Causes his knees to shake, his strength of hands grow less.
But he that has a loving wife,
Him surely does the Lord caress.

XLVIII

An evil wife is a yoke that rubs now to, now fro,
He who has hold of her the scorpion's sting shall know.
A drinking, gadder-round-about
Will all her shame the people show.

XLIX

Three things you rightly fear: the slander of a town,
An angry multitude that surges up and down,
An accusation that is false,
And fourth, a jealous woman's frown.

L

A pleasant wife who will her household duties ply
Is like unto the sun at noon in heaven high.
She fattens up her husband's bones.
Her beauty will he glorify.

LI

As golden pillars set on silver counterpart,
So are the comely feet that bear a faithful heart.
How beautiful the feet of her
Who from the path will not depart!

LII

The tender beauty of her face in ripened age
Is light of candlesticks that does the night assuage.
Night comes. Kindly is fate, if two
Times slowly thickening darkness gauge.

LIII

A sparkling, cheerful tongue will kindly greetings breed.
Of multitudes of friends sweet language is the seed.
Remain at peace with many, but
One counsellor in a thousand heed.

LIV

A man is judged by his walk, his look of peace or scorn,
His laughter, clothes, and how he does himself adorn.
Since few can know your inner worth,
Carry yourself as one well-born.

LV

Seek counsel, but trust your own soul in the dark hour;
Naught is more true to you, or knows as well your power.
Oft times it can see more than seven
Watchmen sitting in a tower.

LVI

To every mighty man be not a ready tool;
Nor make yourself an underling unto a fool;
Nor silly with your servants be,
Nor yet a lion in your rule.

LVII

Is your heart big to hold a love for all? Beware!
Before a stranger lay your secret heart not bare,
Lest by a clever turn or two
He hole you in an ugly snare.

LVIII

Trust none with what you have, lest he become a foe.
Ah see! Here comes a man quite humble, crouching low.
Wipe him as dust upon a glass,
Lest he displace you ere you know.

LIX

Why pity serpent charmers bitten by a snake?
And you, if evil men of you a plaything make?
Will not an earthen pot if dashed
Against an iron kettle break?

LX

He kisses soft your hand. His eyes he has just dried.
'Ah, sir, a little loan,' his purse he opens wide.
You loan... Poor fool! Your money gone,
You have an enemy beside.

LXI

How many great estates has suretyship undone!
How many people suretyship from home has run,
To live and weep in cities strange,
Bereft of what their toil had won!

LXII

Take not the stony way, perchance you be upset.
Watch well the highways where no obstacles are met.
Seek counsel ere you act. When once
The thing is done have no regret.

LXIII

Be noble when you meet your neighbour in his walk,
Not double-tongued like the thief, nor foolish like the gawk;
And winnow not with every wind;
Both shame and honor are in talk.

LXIV

You hear some talk? Keep it, you will not burst and die;
And as one wounded jerks an arrow from his thigh,
So slippery, whispered words outside
The belly of a fool will fly.

LXV

Believe not everything. Most run-down slanders fail.
Admonish a gossip ere your threat make him turn pale;
For everybody talks too much.
So wise, believe not every tale.

LXVI

Now beautiful is speech! But silence is more fair.
Ill does the friendship of a ceaseless talker wear;
For words must nicely fit the time;
But babblers babble without care.

LXVII

The lips of gossips must some mighty tale impart.
A wise man's words are few. He makes of speech an art.
The hearts of fools are in their mouths.
A wise man's mouth is in his heart.

LXVIII

A prudent man with thorny hedge his fence equips,
And binds his money in a bag that never rips;
His speech is slow, he weighs his words,
He makes a door to fit his lips.

LXIX

Truly love your time-tried friend, guard his secrets well,
Lest he escape your snare as does a young gazelle.
No hope at all there is for him
Who itches madly till he tell.

LXX

Stripes mark the tender flesh where swift the whip is
                                      swung;
But bones are scarred and broken where hot words are
                                      flung.
Ah, many fall by the keen sword's edge!
But more have fallen by the tongue.

LXXI

O counsellors, double-tongued, what pleasure you enjoy!
You stir the innocent, the mad to flames decoy,
O'erthrow the houses of the great,
Strong cities plunder and destroy.

LXXII

Measure your friend. Perhaps he is a table friend,
Who will for food and drink your maidens boldly send.
Ah, more faithful, time-hied friend
Both medicine and treasure blend!

LXXIII

Forsake no old-time friend you have found good and true.
Within one's life how many come thy heart to woo
With better drink that stings the tongue!
Far better is old wine than new.

LXXIV

Better reprove your friend, if he has used you ill,
Then silent to remain and harbour anger still.
If he confess his fault, rejoice,
Cleave fast to him with all you will.

LXXV

Be good to your friend. No miser be, although you save.
You soon will leave what gold to you good fortune gave.
You will not need your money then,
There are no dainties in the grave.

LXXVI

In prosperous days how can a man tell who's his friend?
His enemies in secret hate, yet greetings send.
Halt! Fate puffs out as evil wind.
Enemies laugh and friendships end.

LXXVII

A son marred ere his birth can only be a fool.
He always came out empty-headed from his school,
Containing nothing all his days,
A broken vessel by a pool.

LXXVIII

Who builds his house with money of another man,
He widens out a gap that he can never span,
He gathers stones to make his tomb,
He hides in his last caravan.

LXXIX

A fool has soon his foot within his neighbor's gate.
Though hidden soon, a man of wisdom enters late.
A fool will peep in at the door,
A wise man calmly stand and wait.

LXXX

Every thought of a foolish man is but a whim.
His thinking rotates like a rolling axle-rim.
The fool is like the stallion horse,
He neighs whoever sits on him.

LXXXI

To him who has no sense, untruth like truth will seem.
He runs to catch the winds, pursues each golden gleam.
He sleeps and tosses, seeing things,
He flies upon the wings of dreams.

LXXXII

Awake, you fool! Untruth to truth cannot give birth.
Of unclean things can come no cleanly thing of worth.
Give fancies to the wind. Truth needs
No kiss. This is the solid earth.

LXXXIII

The conversation of a fool is mixed and vile,
It is a fallen house heaped up into a pile.
The laughter of a fool is shrill;
A wise man will a little smile.

LXXXIV

Who tries to teach a fool but glues a broken pot.
Beware of fools, lest foolery your virtue blot.
Woe unto you, your peace is gone,
If with a fool you cast your lot!

LXXXV

Weep for the dead, for they have lost the sun's dear light;
Yet dry your eyes, they are asleep in peaceful night.
If you will weep, weep for the fool;
He walks about yet has not sight.

LXXXVI

Go after wisdom; from her footsteps never shrink.
She is a cooling shelter by a river's brink.
See how confounded is the fool;
The fool has never learned to think.

LXXXVII

If you have gathered nothing in the time of youth,
Your later years can be but lonely, sad, uncouth.
Experience is the crown of age.
How comely to gray hair is truth!

LXXXVIII

Be cheerful when ill-fortune swift strikes you a blow,
And patient when your name and your estate are low.
As gold is tried in hottest fire,
Ill-fortune you yourself will show.

LXXXIX

Praise not yourself until your soul be vainly full,
Else will your soul be torn to pieces as a bull;
Or loose its fruit a tree that's dry,
From which you will no olive pull.

XC

Do not puff up yourself in time of some distress.
Far better he that toils and has abundant mess,
Than he that boasts his virtue much,
And every day has less and less.

XCI

Boast not of your possessions round about the town,
Nor when great honor comes upon the lowly frown;
For some who squatted on the earth
Have placed upon their heads a crown.

XCII

Say not. 'I have much goods, what ill can come to me!'
In prosperous days of evil days the memories flee,
And evil days forget past joys.
Our fortunes make the world we see.

XCIII

Oft times a gift brings loss, and glory causes hate.
Somehow o'ernight one rises up from low estate.
Those things we know not why nor how.
Be patient with the hand of fate.

XCIV

How many mighty men have come to naught ere long,
Whose names, disgraced, have mingled with the drunkards'
song!
Time changes; with it all things change,
E'en you and I amid the throng.

XCV

Stuff not yourself with dainty foods until you sigh.
With too much meat you should yourself not stupefy.
For sweets and meats bring sickness, colic.
Ah, many at the table die!

XCVI

The Lord created medicine out of the ground;
And raised up skilled physicians, learned, profound.
Send out for one when you are stuffed
And groaning to your couch are bound.

XCVII

How rich the healthy poor who food and more food crave!
How poor the rich who are a sickly stomach's slave!
Sweets to a shut-up mouth are like
A mess of meat set on a grave.

XCVIII

Remove your mind from heaviness that on it weighs,
From self-accusing thought which like a whiplash flays;
For gladness is the life of man,
And joyfulness prolongs his days.

XCIX

Love your own heart, your comforter yourself shall be;
For sorrow has killed many. The prudent from it flee.
It has no profit for a man.
Hide it away where none can see.

C

Envy and wrath are deadly as a poisonous sting;
And worry pushes autumn in while yet 'tis spring.
But a good and cheerful heart
Will excellent digestion bring.

CI

Anxiety for riches withers up the flesh.
Who has the care thereof the night will not refresh.
How many men has money slain?
Now many strangled in it mesh!

CII

A little food suffices for a man well fed.
He neither groans nor gasps for breath upon his bed.
He rises early in the morning,
His wits are dancing in his head.

CIII

What joy in life is left a man who has no wine?
The grape brings cheer, it will not let the heart repine.
If drunk in moderation only
Gladness blooms upon the vine.

CIV

Your neighbour at the feast you should not taunt or fret;
Nor press upon him that he pay you back a debt.
More caution still; laugh at his jests,
When once his mouth with wine is wet.

CV

Wine drunken to excess exasperates the mind,
Turns loose the rage of fools till they offences find,
Brawling, quarrelling. O many has
It early to the ground consigned!

CVI

At the feast when you are entertaining many a guest,
Lead not the talking, be not over-manifest,
See well-supplied the wants of all,
Sit down, be merry with the rest.

CVII

As flaming sapphire signet set in gold will shine,
So lovely music at a pleasant feast of wine.
Hurt not the sound with useless talk;
But listen whilst you drink and dine.

CVIII

Physicians come, and as they ponder life takes wings;
And they are past and gone who yesterday were kings.
And when a man is dead he but
Inherits worms and creeping things.

CIX

By wariness and pinching one grows very rich;
He says, 'Now will I strut and fill a glorious niche.'
And then there comes a wind and chill,
And he is cast into a ditch.

CX

Be gentle with yourself. Flesh withers fast away.
As leaves, some grow, some fall, each has his day.
Man's work is like unto a wind;
Scarce longer does the worker stay.

CXI

For what is man? And to what purpose labors he?
What is his good? And what the evil he would flee?
At best he has an hundred years,
A sand grain in eternity.

CXII

When full, remembrance keen of hunger do not shun.
When rich, remember all the poor beneath the sun.
Times changes from morning until night;
All things end and are quickly done.

CXIII

Who casts a stone on high shall feel it on his pate.
Who digs a pit, to fall therein shall be his fate.
Remember death, how near it is.
You have no time wherein to hate.

CXIV

Weep, weep, let tears fall over the beloved dead.
Upon his body let the earth be gently spread.
Then cease to weep. You cannot bring
Him back, though seas of tears you shed.

CXV

When you have finished with your tears, let sorrow be.
It does not help the dead. To cheerfulness then flee,
Remembering how brief is life;
Yesterday they, tomorrow we.

CXVI

How many great travails are made for every man!
He carries heavy, galling yokes; his years they span,
From the morn outside his mother's womb
Until his evening caravan.

CXVII

The fear of coming ill, the fear of death's sure thrust,
Trouble men's hearts, and dill their thinking with mistrust-
The same for him upon the throne
And him that's squatting in the dust.

CXVIII

As man grows older, fear and trouble on him creep;
And envy, wrath and strife all day beside him keep;
And in his time of rest at night,
Unpleasant dreams distress his sleep.

CXVIX

Little or nothing is his rest, for in his dream
He keeps the watch in battle, hearing wounded scream.
His heart is troubled, as in sleep
He swims across a bloody stream.

CXX

Distribute not your goods, but firmly hold the key,
Whilst you have breath. From alms of son and wife keep
free.
O piteous age that stretches out
The palm and crooks the beggar's knee!

CXXI

In what you do keep to yourself the upper hand.
O'er your own goods and honor keep a firm command.
When your last days come, there will be time
Enough your fortune to disband.

CXXII

O death, how bitter is the thought that thou art fate,
To him who rests so pleasantly on his estate,
Who prospered in all things, and still
Relishes the food upon his plate!

CXXIII

O death, how welcome to the sick that shake with cold,
And the ragged one that squats in rust and mold,
The troubled, wearied, and the vexed,
And unto him that had grown old!

CXXIV

Remember them that have already paid the score,
And them that still shall pay – yes, more and more.
It is the way of bone and flesh.
Fear not what all have done before.

CXXV

Why will you cry aloud and wet your face with tears?
There is no inquisition in the grave that hears
Or cares how long years sojourn – ten
An hundred, or a thousand years.

CXXVI

Man sadly looks upon the heavens starry bright;
And wistfully he wonders at the sun's dear light.
He knows that he is earth and ashes
That out of beauty soon take flight.

CXXVII

The years have made me full of what I have revealed,
As oft the moon is full. Unto my counsel yield;
Bud forth as roses growing up
Beside a brooklet in a field.

CXXVIII

Some sweetness as of frankincense your lives may hold,
And flourish as the lily when her leaves unfold.
Profit by my counsel, for you
Will know its truth ere you are old.

Note on the text

The original typescript which I have used to produce *Worldy Wisdom Revisited*, Max Ehrmann amended by hand. In the main,, his alterations were a simple substitution of archaic *'thees and thous'*, *'haths and doeths'*, *'thees and thys'*, for the modern equivalents. He elected, however, to retain a number of *'Os, Woes'* and *'Ahs'*. Presumably, he felt this was a balancing act, between retaining the flavor of the original, while not overburdening his reader with too many archaisms.

Most of the remaining revisions were minor and were often concerned with the cadence or rhythm of a line. The changes are often in the nature of adding an adjective (or adverb), so *'pursueth every gleam'* becomes *'pursues each golden gleam'*, or he changes the word order from, for example, *'be no miser'* to *'no miser be'*.

When he marked up the typescript, it seems likely the poem was in its last draft, and, more or less, ready for the printers. Given this, only very rarely was there a strong or substantial change of meaning made to a line. The three alternative line readings below represent pretty much all there is of interest in this regard:*

'…thy strength thou shouldst not plot' altered to *'…your mind and muscle never plot.'* (XI)

'Let dreams and quietness be thine' altered to *'But listen whilst you drink and dine.'* (CVII)

'…whilst thou hast breath in thee' altered to *'…but firmly hold the key.'* (CXX).

APPENDIX

ECCLESIASTES

From *The King James Bible*

The words of the Preacher, the son of David, king in Jerusalem.

Vanity of vanities, saith the Preacher, vanity of vanities; all is vanity.

What profit hath a man of all his labour which he taketh under the sun?

One generation passeth away, and another generation cometh; but the earth abideth forever.

The sun also ariseth, and the sun goeth down, and hasteth to his place where he arose.

The wind goeth toward the south, and turneth about unto the north; it whirleth about continually, and the wind returneth again according to his circuits.

All the rivers run into the sea; yet the sea is not full; unto place from whence the rivers come, thither they return again.

All things are full of labour; man cannot utter it; the eye is not satisfied with seeing, nor the ear filled with hearing.

The thing that hath been, it is that which shall be; and that which is done is that which shall be done; and there is no new thing under the sun.

Is there anything whereof it may be said, 'See, this is new?' It hath been already of old time, which was before us.

There is no remembrance of former things; neither shall there be any remembrance of things that are to come with those that shall come after.

I the Preacher was king over Israel in Jerusalem.

And I gave my heart to seek and search out by wisdom concerning all things that are done under heaven; this sore travail hath God given to the sons of man to be exercised therewith.

I have seen all the works that are done under the sun; and, behold, all is vanity and vexation of spirit.

That which is crooked cannot be made straight; and that which is wanting cannot be numbered.

I communed with mine own heart, saying, 'Lo, I am come to great estate, and have gotten more wisdom than all they that have been before me in Jerusalem;' yea, my heart had great experience of wisdom and knowledge.

And I gave my heart to know wisdom, and to know madness and folly; I perceived that this also is vexation of spirit.

For in much wisdom is much grief; and he that increaseth knowledge increaseth sorrow.

I said in mine heart, 'Go to now, I will prove thee with mirth, therefore enjoy pleasure;' and, behold, this also is vanity.

I said of laughter, 'It is mad; and of mirth, What doeth it?'

I sought in mine heart to give myself unto wine, yet acquainting mine heart with wisdom; and to lay hold on folly, till I might see what was that good for the sons of men, which they should do under the heaven all the days of their life.

I made me great works; I builded me houses; I planted me vineyards;

I made me gardens and orchards, and I planted trees in them of all kind of fruits;

I made me pools of water, to water therewith the wood that bringeth forth trees;

I got me servants and maidens, and had servants born in my house; also I had great possessions of great and small cattle above all that were in Jerusalem before me;

I gathered me also silver and gold, and the peculiar treasure of kings and of the provinces; I gat me men singers and women singers, and the delights of the sons of men, as musical instruments, and that of all sorts.

So I was great, and increased more than all that were before me in Jerusalem; also my wisdom remained with me.

And whatsoever mine eyes desired I kept not from them, I withheld not my heart from any joy; for my heart rejoiced in all my labour; and this was my portion of all my labour.

Then I looked on all the works that my hands had wrought, and on the labour that I had laboured to do; and, behold, all was vanity and vexation of spirit, and there was no profit under the sun.

And I turned myself to behold wisdom, and madness, and folly; for what can the man do that cometh after the king? Even that which hath been already done.

Then I saw that wisdom excelleth folly, as far as light excelleth darkness.

The wise man's eyes are in his head; but the fool walketh in darkness; and I myself perceived also that one event happeneth to them all.

Then said I in my heart, as it happeneth to the fool, so it happeneth even to me; and why was I then more wise? Then I said in my heart, that this also is vanity.

For there is no remembrance of the wise more than of the fool for ever; seeing that which now is in the days to come shall all be forgotten. And how dieth the wise man? As the fool.

Therefore I hated life; because the work that is wrought under the sun is grievous unto me; for all is vanity and vexation of spirit.

Yea, I hated all my labour which I had taken under the sun; because I should leave it unto the man that shall be after me.

And who knoweth whether he shall be a wise man or a fool? Yet shall he have rule over all my labour wherein I have laboured, and wherein I have shewed myself wise under the sun. This is also vanity.

Therefore I went about to cause my heart to despair of all the labour which I took under the sun.

For there is a man whose labour is in wisdom, and in knowledge, and in equity; yet to a man that hath not laboured therein shall he leave it for his portion. This also is vanity and a great evil.

For what hath man of all his labour, and of the vexation of his heart, wherein he hath laboured under the sun?

For all his days are sorrows, and his travail grief; yea, his heart taketh not rest in the night. This is also vanity.

There is nothing better for a man, than that he should eat and drink, and that he should make his soul enjoy good in his labour. This also I saw, that it was from the hand of God.

For who can eat, or who else can hasten hereunto, more

than I?

For God giveth to a man that is good in his sight wisdom, and knowledge, and joy; but to the sinner he giveth travail, to gather and to heap up, that he may give to him that is good before God. This also is vanity and vexation of spirit.

To everything there is a season, and a time to every purpose under the heaven;

A time to be born, and a time to die; a time to plant, and a time to pluck up that which is planted;

A time to kill, and a time to heal; a time to break down, and a time to build up;

A time to weep, and a time to laugh; a time to mourn, and a time to dance;

A time to cast away stones, and a time to gather stones together; a time to embrace, and a time to refrain from embracing;

A time to get, and a time to lose; a time to keep, and a time to cast away;

A time to rend, and a time to sew; a time to keep silence, and a time to speak;

A time to love, and a time to hate; a time of war, and a time of peace.

What profit hath he that worketh in that wherein he

laboureth?

I have seen the travail, which God hath given to the sons of men to be exercised in it.

He hath made everything beautiful in his time; also he hath set the world in their heart, so that no man can find out the work that God maketh from the beginning to the end.

I know that there is no good in them, but for a man to rejoice, and to do good in his life.

And also that every man should eat and drink, and enjoy the good of all his labour, it is the gift of God.

I know that, whatsoever God doeth, it shall be forever; nothing can be put to it, nor anything taken from it; and God doeth it, that men should fear before him.

That which hath been is now; and that which is to be hath already been; and God requireth that which is past.

And moreover I saw under the sun the place of judgment, that wickedness was there; and the place of righteousness, that iniquity was there.

I said in mine heart, God shall judge the righteous and the wicked; for there is a time there for every purpose and for every work.

I said in mine heart concerning the estate of the sons of men, that God might manifest them, and that they might see that they themselves are beasts.

For that which befalleth the sons of men befalleth beasts; even one thing befalleth them; as the one dieth, so dieth the other; yea, they have all one breath; so that a man hath no pre-eminence above a beast; for all is vanity.

All go unto one place; all are of the dust, and all turn to dust again.

Who knoweth the spirit of man that goeth upward, and the spirit of the beast that goeth downward to the earth?

Wherefore I perceive that there is nothing better, than that a man should rejoice in his own works; for that is his portion; for who shall bring him to see what shall be after him?

So I returned, and considered all the oppressions that are done under the sun; and behold the tears of such as were oppressed, and they had no comforter; and on the side of their oppressors there was power; but they had no comforter.

Wherefore I praised the dead which are already dead more than the living which are yet alive.

Yea, better is he than both they, which hath not yet been, who hath not seen the evil work that is done under the sun.

Again, I considered all travail, and every right work, that for this a man is envied of his neighbour. This is also vanity and vexation of spirit.

The fool foldeth his hands together, and eateth his own

flesh.

Better is an handful with quietness, than both the hands full with travail and vexation of spirit.

Then I returned, and I saw vanity under the sun.

There is one alone, and there is not a second; yea, he hath neither child nor brother; yet is there no end of all his labour; neither is his eye satisfied with riches; neither saith he, for whom do I labour, and bereave my soul of good? This is also vanity, yea, it is a sore travail.

Two are better than one; because they have a good reward for their labour.

For if they fall, the one will lift up his fellow; but woe to him that is alone when he falleth; for he hath not another to help him up.

Again, if two lie together, then they have heat; but how can one be warm alone?

And if one prevail against him, two shall withstand him; and a threefold cord is not quickly broken.

Better is a poor and a wise child than an old and foolish king, who will no more be admonished.

For out of prison he cometh to reign; whereas also he that is born in his kingdom becometh poor.

I considered all the living which walk under the sun, with

the second child that shall stand up in his stead.

There is no end of all the people, even of all that have been before them; they also that come after shall not rejoice in him. Surely this also is vanity and vexation of spirit.

Keep thy foot when thou goest to the house of God, and be more ready to hear, than to give the sacrifice of fools; for they consider not that they do evil.

Be not rash with thy mouth, and let not thine heart be hasty to utter anything before God; for God is in heaven, and thou upon earth; therefore let thy words be few.

For a dream cometh through the multitude of business; and a fool's voice is known by multitude of words.

When thou vowest a vow unto God, defer not to pay it; for he hath no pleasure in fools; pay that which thou hast vowed.

Better is it that thou shouldest not vow, than that thou shouldest vow and not pay.

Suffer not thy mouth to cause thy flesh to sin; neither say thou before the angel, that it was an error; wherefore should God be angry at thy voice, and destroy the work of thine hands?

For in the multitude of dreams and many words there are also divers vanities; but fear thou God.

If thou seest the oppression of the poor, and violent

perverting of judgment and justice in a province, marvel not at the matter; for he that is higher than the highest regardeth; and there be higher than they.

Moreover the profit of the earth is for all; the king himself is served by the field.

He that loveth silver shall not be satisfied with silver; nor he that loveth abundance with increase; this is also vanity.

When goods increase, they are increased that eat them; and what good is there to the owners thereof, saving the beholding of them with their eyes?

The sleep of a labouring man is sweet, whether he eat little or much; but the abundance of the rich will not suffer him to sleep.

There is a sore evil which I have seen under the sun, namely, riches kept for the owners thereof to their hurt.

But those riches perish by evil travail; and he begetteth a son, and there is nothing in his hand.

As he came forth of his mother's womb, naked shall he return to go as he came, and shall take nothing of his labour, which he may carry away in his hand.

And this also is a sore evil, that in all points as he came, so shall he go; and what profit hath he that hath laboured for the wind?

All his days also he eateth in darkness, and he hath much

sorrow and wrath with his sickness.

Behold that which I have seen; it is good and comely for one to eat and to drink, and to enjoy the good of all his labour that he taketh under the sun all the days of his life, which God giveth him; for it is his portion.

Every man also to whom God hath given riches and wealth, and hath given him power to eat thereof, and to take his portion, and to rejoice in his labour; this is the gift of God.

For he shall not much remember the days of his life; because God answereth him in the joy of his heart.

There is an evil which I have seen under the sun, and it is common among men;

A man to whom God hath given riches, wealth, and honour, so that he wanteth nothing for his soul of all that he desireth, yet God giveth him not power to eat thereof, but a stranger eateth it; this is vanity, and it is an evil disease.

If a man beget an hundred children, and live many years, so that the days of his years be many, and his soul be not filled with good, and also that he have no burial; I say, that an untimely birth is better than he.

For he cometh in with vanity, and departeth in darkness, and his name shall be covered with darkness.

Moreover he hath not seen the sun, nor known anything;

this hath more rest than the other.

Yea, though he live a thousand years twice told, yet hath he seen no good; do not all go to one place?

All the labour of man is for his mouth, and yet the appetite is not filled.

For what hath the wise more than the fool? What hath the poor that knoweth to walk before the living?

Better is the sight of the eyes than the wandering of the desire; this is also vanity and vexation of spirit.

That which hath been is named already, and it is known that it is man; neither may he contend with him that is mightier than he.

Seeing there be many things that increase vanity, what is man the better?

For who knoweth what is good for man in this life, all the days of his vain life which he spendeth as a shadow? For who can tell a man what shall be after him under the sun?

A good name is better than precious ointment; and the day of death than the day of one's birth.

It is better to go to the house of mourning, than to go to the house of feasting; for that is the end of all men; and the living will lay it to his heart.

Sorrow is better than laughter; for by the sadness of the

countenance the heart is made better.

The heart of the wise is in the house of mourning; but the heart of fools is in the house of mirth.

It is better to hear the rebuke of the wise, than for a man to hear the song of fools.

For as the crackling of thorns under a pot, so is the laughter of the fool; this also is vanity.

Surely oppression maketh a wise man mad; and a gift destroyeth the heart.

Better is the end of a thing than the beginning thereof; and the patient in spirit is better than the proud in spirit.

Be not hasty in thy spirit to be angry; for anger resteth in the bosom of fools.

Say not thou, what is the cause that the former days were better than these? For thou dost not enquire wisely concerning this.

Wisdom is good with an inheritance; and by it there is profit to them that see the sun.

For wisdom is a defence, and money is a defence; but the excellency of knowledge is, that wisdom giveth life to them that have it.

Consider the work of God; for who can make that straight, which he hath made crooked?

In the day of prosperity be joyful, but in the day of adversity consider; God also hath set the one over against the other, to the end that man should find nothing after him.

All things have I seen in the days of my vanity; there is a just man that perisheth in his righteousness, and there is a wicked man that prolongeth his life in his wickedness.

Be not righteous over much; neither make thyself over wise; why shouldest thou destroy thyself?

Be not over much wicked, neither be thou foolish; why shouldest thou die before thy time?

It is good that thou shouldest take hold of this; yea, also from this withdraw not thine hand; for he that feareth God shall come forth of them all.

Wisdom strengtheneth the wise more than ten mighty men which are in the city.

For there is not a just man upon earth, that doeth good, and sinneth not.

Also take no heed unto all words that are spoken; lest thou hear thy servant curse thee;

For oftentimes also thine own heart knoweth that thou thyself likewise hast cursed others.

'All this have I proved by wisdom;' I said, I will be wise; but it was far from me.

That which is far off, and exceeding deep, who can find it out?

I applied mine heart to know, and to search, and to seek out wisdom, and the reason of things, and to know the wickedness of folly, even of foolishness and madness;

And I find more bitter than death the woman, whose heart is snares and nets, and her hands as bands; whoso pleaseth God shall escape from her; but the sinner shall be taken by her.

'Behold, this have I found' saith the preacher, counting one by one, to find out the account;

Which yet my soul seeketh, but I find not; one man among a thousand have I found; but a woman among all those have I not found.

Lo, this only have I found, that God hath made man upright; but they have sought out many inventions.

Who is as the wise man? And who knoweth the interpretation of a thing? A man's wisdom maketh his face to shine, and the boldness of his face shall be changed.

I counsel thee to keep the king's commandment, and that in regard of the oath of God.

Be not hasty to go out of his sight; stand not in an evil thing; for he doeth whatsoever pleaseth him.

Where the word of a king is, there is power; and who may

say unto him, 'What doest thou?'

Whoso keepeth the commandment shall feel no evil thing; and a wise man's heart discerneth both time and judgment.

Because to every purpose there is time and judgment, therefore the misery of man is great upon him.

For he knoweth not that which shall be; for who can tell him when it shall be?

There is no man that hath power over the spirit to retain the spirit; neither hath he power in the day of death; and there is no discharge in that war; neither shall wickedness deliver those that are given to it.

All this have I seen, and applied my heart unto every work that is done under the sun; there is a time wherein one man ruleth over another to his own hurt.

And so I saw the wicked buried, who had come and gone from the place of the holy, and they were forgotten in the city where they had so done; this is also vanity.

Because sentence against an evil work is not executed speedily, therefore the heart of the sons of men is fully set in them to do evil.

Though a sinner do evil an hundred times, and his days be prolonged, yet surely I know that it shall be well with them that fear God, which fear before him;

But it shall not be well with the wicked, neither shall he

prolong his days, which are as a shadow; because he feareth not before God.

There is a vanity which is done upon the earth; that there be just men, unto whom it happeneth according to the work of the wicked; again, there be wicked men, to whom it happeneth according to the work of the righteous; I said that this also is vanity.

Then I commended mirth, because a man hath no better thing under the sun, than to eat, and to drink, and to be merry; for that shall abide with him of his labour the days of his life, which God giveth him under the sun.

When I applied mine heart to know wisdom, and to see the business that is done upon the earth; (for also there is that neither day nor night seeth sleep with his eyes) then I beheld all the work of God, that a man cannot find out the work that is done under the sun; because though a man labour to seek it out, yet he shall not find it; yea farther; though a wise man think to know it, yet shall he not be able to find it.

For all this I considered in my heart even to declare all this, that the righteous, and the wise, and their works, are in the hand of God; no man knoweth either love or hatred by all that is before them.

All things come alike to all; there is one event to the righteous, and to the wicked; to the good and to the clean, and to the unclean; to him that sacrificeth, and to him that sacrificeth not; as is the good, so is the sinner; and he that sweareth, as he that feareth an oath.

This is an evil among all things that are done under the sun, that there is one event unto all; yea, also the heart of the sons of men is full of evil, and madness is in their heart while they live, and after that they go to the dead.

For to him that is joined to all the living there is hope; for a living dog is better than a dead lion.

For the living know that they shall die; but the dead know not anything, neither have they any more a reward; for the memory of them is forgotten.

Also their love, and their hatred, and their envy, is now perished; neither have they any more a portion forever in anything that is done under the sun.

Go thy way, eat thy bread with joy, and drink thy wine with a merry heart; for God now accepteth thy works.

Let thy garments be always white; and let thy head lack no ointment.

Live joyfully with the wife whom thou lovest all the days of the life of thy vanity, which he hath given thee under the sun, all the days of thy vanity; for that is thy portion in this life, and in thy labour which thou takest under the sun.

Whatsoever thy hand findeth to do, do it with thy might; for there is no work, nor device, nor knowledge, nor wisdom, in the grave, whither thou goest.

I returned, and saw under the sun, that the race is not to the swift, nor the battle to the strong, neither yet bread to the wise, nor yet riches to men of understanding, nor yet favour to men of skill; but time and chance happeneth to them all.

For man also knoweth not his time; as the fishes that are taken in an evil net, and as the birds that are caught in the snare; so are the sons of men snared in an evil time, when it falleth suddenly upon them.

This wisdom have I seen also under the sun, and it seemed great unto me;

There was a little city, and few men within it; and there came a great king against it, and besieged it, and built great bulwarks against it;

Now there was found in it a poor wise man, and he by his wisdom delivered the city; yet no man remembered that same poor man.

Then said I, Wisdom is better than strength; nevertheless the poor man's wisdom is despised, and his words are not heard.

The words of wise men are heard in quiet more than the cry of him that ruleth among fools.

Wisdom is better than weapons of war; but one sinner destroyeth much good.

Dead flies cause the ointment of the apothecary to send forth a stinking savour; so doth a little folly him that is in reputation for wisdom and honour.

A wise man's heart is at his right hand; but a fool's heart at his left.

Yea also, when he that is a fool walketh by the way, his wisdom faileth him, and he saith to everyone that he is a fool.

If the spirit of the ruler rise up against thee, leave not thy place; for yielding pacifieth great offences.

There is an evil which I have seen under the sun, as an error which proceedeth from the ruler;

Folly is set in great dignity, and the rich sit in low place.

I have seen servants upon horses, and princes walking as servants upon the earth.

He that diggeth a pit shall fall into it; and whoso breaketh an hedge, a serpent shall bite him.

Whoso removeth stones shall be hurt therewith; and he that cleaveth wood shall be endangered thereby.

If the iron be blunt, and he do not whet the edge, then must he put to more strength; but wisdom is profitable to direct.

Surely the serpent will bite without enchantment; and a babbler is no better.

The words of a wise man's mouth are gracious; but the lips of a fool will swallow up himself.

The beginning of the words of his mouth is foolishness; and the end of his talk is mischievous madness.

A fool also is full of words; a man cannot tell what shall be; and what shall be after him, who can tell him?

The labour of the foolish wearieth every one of them, because he knoweth not how to go to the city.

Woe to thee, O land, when thy king is a child, and thy princes eat in the morning!

Blessed art thou, O land, when thy king is the son of nobles, and thy princes eat in due season, for strength, and not for drunkenness!

By much slothfulness the building decayeth; and through idleness of the hands the house droppeth through.

A feast is made for laughter, and wine maketh merry; but money answereth all things.

Curse not the king, no not in thy thought; and curse not the rich in thy bedchamber; for a bird of the air shall carry the voice, and that which hath wings shall tell the matter.

Cast thy bread upon the waters; for thou shalt find it after many days.

Give a portion to seven, and also to eight; for thou knowest not what evil shall be upon the earth.

If the clouds be full of rain, they empty themselves upon

the earth; and if the tree fall toward the south, or toward the north, in the place where the tree falleth, there it shall be.

He that observeth the wind shall not sow; and he that regardeth the clouds shall not reap.

As thou knowest not what is the way of the spirit, nor how the bones do grow in the womb of her that is with child; even so thou knowest not the works of God who maketh all.

In the morning sow thy seed, and in the evening withhold not thine hand; for thou knowest not whether shall prosper, either this or that, or whether they both shall be alike good.

Truly the light is sweet, and a pleasant thing it is for the eyes to behold the sun;

But if a man live many years, and rejoice in them all; yet let him remember the days of darkness; for they shall be many. All that cometh is vanity.

Rejoice, O young man, in thy youth; and let thy heart cheer thee in the days of thy youth, and walk in the ways of thine heart, and in the sight of thine eyes; but know thou, that for all these things God will bring thee into judgment.

Therefore remove sorrow from thy heart, and put away evil from thy flesh; for childhood and youth are vanity.

Remember now thy Creator in the days of thy youth, while

the evil days come not, nor the years draw nigh, when thou shalt say, I have no pleasure in them;

While the sun, or the light, or the moon, or the stars, be not darkened, nor the clouds return after the rain;

In the day when the keepers of the house shall tremble, and the strong men shall bow themselves, and the grinders cease because they are few, and those that look out of the windows be darkened,

And the doors shall be shut in the streets, when the sound of the grinding is low, and he shall rise up at the voice of the bird, and all the daughters of music shall be brought low;

Also when they shall be afraid of that which is high, and fears shall be in the way, and the almond tree shall flourish, and the grasshopper shall be a burden, and desire shall fail; because man goeth to his long home, and the mourners go about the streets;

Or ever the silver cord be loosed, or the golden bowl be broken, or the pitcher be broken at the fountain, or the wheel broken at the cistern.

Then shall the dust return to the earth as it was; and the spirit shall return unto God who gave it.

Vanity of vanities, saith the preacher; all is vanity.

And moreover, because the preacher was wise, he still taught the people knowledge; yea, he gave good heed, and sought out, and set in order many proverbs.

The preacher sought to find out acceptable words; and that which was written was upright, even words of truth.

The words of the wise are as goads, and as nails fastened by the masters of assemblies, which are given from one shepherd.

And further, by these, my son, be admonished; of making many books there is no end; and much study is a weariness of the flesh.

Let us hear the conclusion of the whole matter; Fear God, and keep his commandments; for this is the whole duty of man.

For God shall bring every work into judgment, with every secret thing, whether it be good, or whether it be evil.

Note: I have taken a few liberties with this very well known version of the biblical text. Firstly, I have removed the 'chapter and verse' numbering, to make the book easier to read and compare, to Ehrmann's reinterpretation. Secondly, I have removed the space between certain words which may distract the contemporary reader, so *'Any thing'* becomes *'Anything'* and *'For ever'* becomes *'Forever'* and so on.

ABOUT THE EDITOR

Tim Dalgleish is the author of two volumes of poetry *The Stones of Mithras* and *Penumbra*, numerous plays and a book on acting called *Playing Macbeth: An Actor's Journey into the Role* (called by reviewers 'A thrilling journey' and a 'Fantastic insider's view'). As an actor he has worked with theatre companies from RAT Theatre to Voices of the Holocaust.

He played Snout in *A Midsummer Night's Dream* as part of the RSC's Open Stages programme and was the lead in *Macbeth* for the Open Theatre Group. He has appeared briefly in several feature films, the most recent being the British-Muslim comedy *Finding Fatimah* and the (soon to be released) gangster movie *Milk and Honey*, he was also in the short film *Imagine* which received Special Mention at the Marbella International Film Festival.

His third collection of essays, *The Three Hearts of the Octopus* was recently published and follows on from two previous collections, *The Purple Rose* and *Orwell, Two Guinea Pigs, A Cat and A Goat*. The most recent book he edited *Lifting the Veil* was also by Max Ehrmann. He regularly narrates audio books, several of the most recent being: *Hamelin's Child* by DJ Bennet and *After Dunkirk: D-Day and How We Planned the Second Front* by Major John Dalgleish (his great uncle). More information at www.lookingfortim.com.

ALSO BY TIM DALGLEISH

Non-Fiction

Scotland before Scotland

Lifting it off the Page

The Guerilla Philosopher

Playing Macbeth: An Actor's Journey into the Role

Poetry

Reflections from Mirror City (anthology)

The Stones of Mithras

Penumbra

Plays

The Last Days of Adam

The Life and Theatre of Antonin Artaud

Essays

The Purple Rose and other essays

Orwell, Two Guinea Pigs, A Cat and A Goat and other essays

The Three Hearts of the Octopus

As Editor

The Rose by WB Yeats

Dracula's Guest by Bram Stoker

The Ballad of Reading Gaol with Humanitad by Oscar Wilde

After Dunkirk by Major John Dalgleish

Lifting the Veil by Max Ehrmann

Printed in Great Britain
by Amazon